# El  Bowie Bakery

By Dr. Toni Viva Muñoz

TCU Press

FORT WORTH, TEXAS

Copyright © 2025 by Dr. Toni Viva Muñoz
Library of Congress Cataloging-in-Publication Data

Names: Muñoz, Toni Viva, 1979- author.
Title: El Bowie Bakery / by Dr. Toni Viva Muñoz.
Description: Fort Worth, Texas : TCU Press, [2025] | Includes
  bibliographical references. | Summary: "As a ninth-generation
  Bordercana, Toni and her family are a mestizo mix of Native American and
  Mexican American heritage. They never left the Border. Growing up, she
  was never made to think of the Border--this in-between space--as two
  different spaces. In this multi-generational nonfiction story, Toni
  retells her abuelos' love story to her young daughters while sharing the
  history of the area and its Latinx people. In La Union, the town where
  her family lives and where their family has always lived, the adobe
  dwellings are made from la tierra. The same earth is a womb for fallen
  ancestors--the Apaches who once roamed the area, the Spaniards who came
  before 1821, the Mexicans who came after, and the Mexican Americans and
  Bordercanx who inhabit the area today. From start to finish, this story
  is the embodiment of a Mexican American, double hybridized population.
  It is among the many stories of people still thriving and not forgotten
  along the US-Mexico. Border"-- Provided by publisher.
Identifiers: LCCN 2024046885 | ISBN 9780875659114
Subjects: LCSH: Muñoz, Toni Viva, 1979---Juvenile literature. | Muñoz
  family--Juvenile literature. | Mestizos--New Mexico--La
  Union--Biography--Juvenile literature. | Grandparent and child--New
  Mexico--La Union--Juvenile literature. | La Union (N.M.)--Social life
  and customs--20th century--Juvenile literature. | La Union
  (N.M.)--Biography--Juvenile literature.
Classification: LCC F804.L26 M86 2025 | DDC 978.9/66 [B]--dc23/eng/20241226
LC record available at https://lccn.loc.gov/2024046885

TCU Box 298300
Fort Worth, Texas 76129
www.tcupress.com

*Layout design by Adrienne Martinez*

This book is dedicated to Darlington and Tennyson.
May our ancestors continue to inspire us and
whisper stories in the wind.

# Acknowledgments

This labor of love would have been impossible without the many collaborators and supporters who have given me their time, insight, expertise, and encouragement throughout my life and academic career.

Ms. Kyle, my fifth-grade teacher, saw my potential, kept me out of trouble, and showed me a path to a better future. Ms. Bradley, my high school sociology teacher, gave me a place to shine and develop creative work effectively. These teachers provided a home for us many misfits, and I am forever grateful for all this initial love and guidance.

For the longest time, I have kept important aspects of my life separate. I was under the impression that they could not work together. However, without one, the other would not exist. Therefore, I am especially indebted to all the members of the fashion industry who opened the door to me as a young teen, giving me a chance at a once-in-a-lifetime opportunity with unlimited possibilities, introducing me to lifelong friendships and collaborators, and providing me with the means to pay for a decade of school without any debt. There have been too many years and too many people to mention here, but without their support, I would not have been at this place in my journey today.

As the only member of my immediate family to receive a bachelor's degree or my extended family to receive a Ph.D., I am profoundly grateful to Dr. Betty Wiesepape and Dr. R. Clay Reynolds for exposing my voice and vulnerabilities. They taught me how to harness these aspects of identity and place and turn them into a passion for creative and scholarly discourse. Their guidance and mentorship have ignited a flame that cannot be extinguished.

Through the years, The University of Texas at Dallas has become my academic home, has supported all my professional goals, and continues to do so. I am especially thankful to Dean Nils Roemer, Dr. Manuel Luis Martinez, Dr. Shilyh Warren, and Dr. Pia Jakobsson for their unwavering dedication to my scholarly and creative work on the U.S.-Mexico Border. I would also like to thank my colleagues, Dr. Nomi Stone and Liz Trospher, for all their love and collaboration.

Additionally, I would like to thank all the publication editors who helped shape and publish each of my short stories and scholarly articles, and specifically, Dr. Tim Walters, for his edits, insights, and knowledge pertaining specifically to my proposal, dissertation, and creative work.

I would also like to give a heartfelt thank you to Dr. Dan Williams of TCU Press for believing in my work and giving me a platform to share it. And to the TCU Press Team, Marco Roc, Adrienne Martinez, and James Lehr, I would like to share my sincere gratitude for your time, talent, and dedication for seeing this project through.

For my creative work, I would like to thank my collaborative team for all of their talent and support—Susie Cortez (painter/illustrator), Simon Lopez (photographer), Taylor Higginbotham (graphic designer), and Melissa Adams (layout designer). As a mother, I would be remiss if I did not thank my babysitter, Delmy Calderon, for allowing me quality time to focus on my work and all my creative endeavors.

I have long since struggled with how to share my inbetweenness as a Bordercanx artist in a way that honors and respects my Border home but also captures the grit, heartache, and beauty of this space. If it were not for artists like Rudolfo Anaya and Denise Chavez, I would not have found my way. I am forever grateful for all those before us and all those who continue to pave the way and be a "bridge to understanding," like my dear friend Sergio Troncoso.

In the pursuing this project, I am particularly grateful for the assistance and constant willingness to receive late-night phone calls from my dear friends, Laura de la Torre and Kathryn Fuller, along with my loving family. I want to thank my abuelos, whose love, guidance, and constant urging me never to forget where I came from continue to inspire my work today, and I am grateful to my parents, my ultimate role models, for their unconditional love. Most importantly, I would like to thank my curious and vivacious girls, Darlington and Tennyson. They are my muses, and I live to make them proud.

Fall in New Mexico is the most miraculous time of year. Miles of unharvested fields stretch as far and wide as the mirroring skies. Giant corn mazes rise from the earth and consume curious **niñas**—like you girls—for hours.

At night, when the desert sun hides behind the moon, sounds of laughter fill the air. Mesquite trees smell like rain and mingle in the aroma of freshly picked corn and chili churning in large metal roasters. This is how we spent our days where your mamá grew up, here along the Rio Grande. Every day in these tiny towns with dirt roads and adobe homes was about being with **familia**.

But growing up, Sundays were especially about **mis Abuelos**.

Maria Refugio Fierro Cruz Muñoz was a great woman with many names and as many friends and relatives. She was a force of goodness. Strong and steady. Still and deeply rooted in her faith and homeland. With hair as dark as a raven's back and skin as smooth as desert dunes, she was a vision to behold.

Everyone from our small town and every small town nearby liked her and called her Cuca. She was born in La Union, like her mamá, and her **abuela**, and her **bisabuela**, and her **tatara abuela**.

And like all the women who came before her, Cuca never missed Mass.

If I made it to Mass early enough, I'd help her ready **Padre's** robe and the small offering baskets lined with dark velvet.

When **Padre** was not at church, he was in **nuestra casa** for **Abuela's** advice, her wonderful stories, and, of course, for her **comida**.

The rich spices of **Chile Colorado, mole, rellenos, menudo,** and **posole**, like a giant sarape weaved their aromas around my memories.

But, **Abuela's** tortillas—straight from **el comal**—were what I lived for. My job was to roll the **masa** into perfect little balls, and **Abuela** shaped them just right with a tiny **plancha**. When we finished, we would spread fresh **mantequilla** over each little round one.

Then, on Sundays, she'd wrap me up tight in her arms, from a *tortilla* to a little *burrito*.

From the warmth of *Abuela's* embrace, I hardly heard *Padre's* words, but like any good *mijita*, I went through the motions—standing, kneeling, sitting.

Because that is what all of us *buenas Catolicas* did, *Abuela* said.

I used to think of myself as a puzzle piece that fits perfectly between the two.

As for **Abuelo**, he towered above the rest of us.

**Abuelo** Poncho was a man of few names and even fewer words and friends. Fair-skinned and lanky, he was like a long twig in a windstorm, with the whitest cotton-candy cloud of hair.

"Look how much taller I am," **Abuelo** would say with a slight smile.

"And look at me, **Abuelo**. I am tall too," I'd say, standing on tippy toes.

"**Sí, Americanos** are tall," he'd say.

"But we are Mexicans, too. Right, **Abuelo**?" I'd ask.

"No, **sólo Americanos**," he always insisted.

"We are both, **Mijita**." **Abuela** would smile at me and shake her head at **Abuelo**.

At school, one of the boys told me that Abuelo had been a sniper in the war.

He put his arms together and made an imaginary rifle. Then, he cocked his head to one side as if he were looking at something in the faraway distance.

He thought that maybe fighting for one country made Abuelo pick one country over two. And maybe this is why Papá didn't like us speaking Spanish when we were not at home. I wondered. Maybe Papá had to pick one country over the other, too.

Most Sundays were the same around here, except those Sundays when **Abuela** left for Mexico on one of her mission trips.

A white school van sputtered up to the front of Our Lady of Refuge. Like **Abuela**, plump, proud women wore straw hats jammed inside, clutching fanny packs and sacks filled with yummy snacks.

Abuela always brought pan dulce from El Bowie Bakery. Through the window, she made the sign of the cross and gave me her blessings of departure, "¡Dios te bendiga!" she said.

In a cloud of dust, I waved goodbye as Abuela y las mujeres were whisked away.

On those Sundays without Abuela, Abuelo did his best to roll me up in his arms like a little burrito. We sat quietly listening to Padre's Mass, and after Mass, we raced back to the house to get Abuelo's truck.

Abuelo treasured his American pickup truck, with partes Americanas by manos Americanas.

But this one particular Sunday, I remember it like yesterday. When we jumped in the old truck, the same golden-brown color as the New Mexico desert, I just knew we were in for an adventure.

On the dashboard of the old truck, tiny cracks spread like arroyos without rain, dry and stretching across over time.

Abuelo and I watched the speedometer needle bounce up and down as we bumped along the dirt road.

When we finally made our way to the paved streets of the city, the speedometer jumped up one last time, but it never came down.

This had us laughing, so much so that by the time we saw the yellow light approaching...

Abuelo's foot could not decide what it wanted to do.

The truck lunged forward and stalled, sending my head into the dashboard and all those little arroyos. A fistful of tears swelled in my throat. I closed my eyes and tried not to cry.

Then, I felt the truck make a giant U-turn.

"Where are we going, Abuelo?" I asked, wiping the sweat from my forehead.

I hated to miss out on our adventure, but when I looked down at the sweat puddles in my lap, I realized they were bright red.

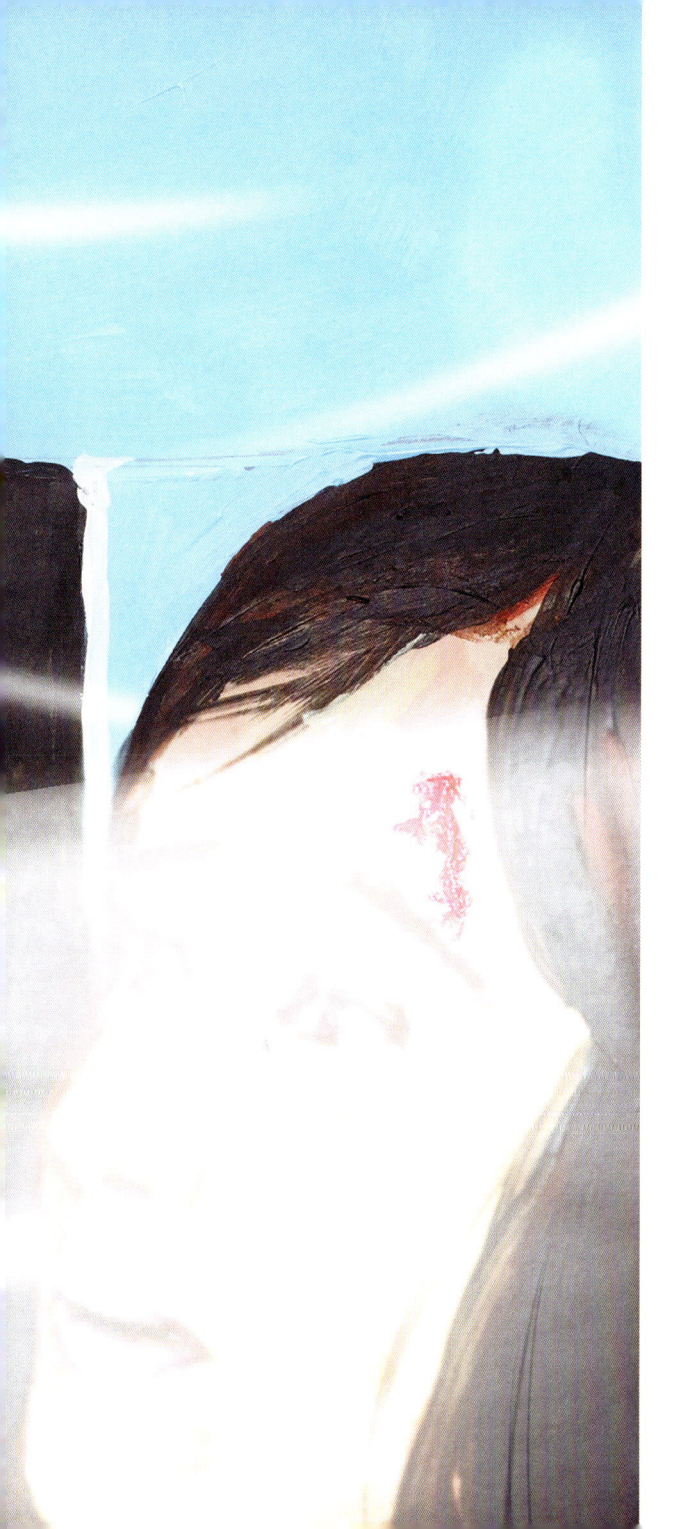

"¡Cálmate!" Abuelo instructed as he held my eyes open and reached for the flashlight from his toolbox.

"¿Qué, Abuelo?" I asked.

"No brain damage." He laughed and poured a splash of alcohol on my cut before I could protest.

"¡Ay!" I yelped, and the tears rolled down my face. Abuelo propped my hands around the cut.

"Here, keep your hands cómo así."

"What's that?" My lips quivered.

**Abuelo** took the tiniest tube between his fingers and opened the cap. The strong odor tickled my nose, and I immediately knew the smell.

"No!" I shouted. "My head will stick like that forever." I had always been warned not to play with Super Glue.

"**Mira, Mijita**, if it's good enough for the U.S. Army..." He steadied his hand.

And just like that, I closed my eyes and stopped squirming. I could not let a little Super Glue stop my big adventure.

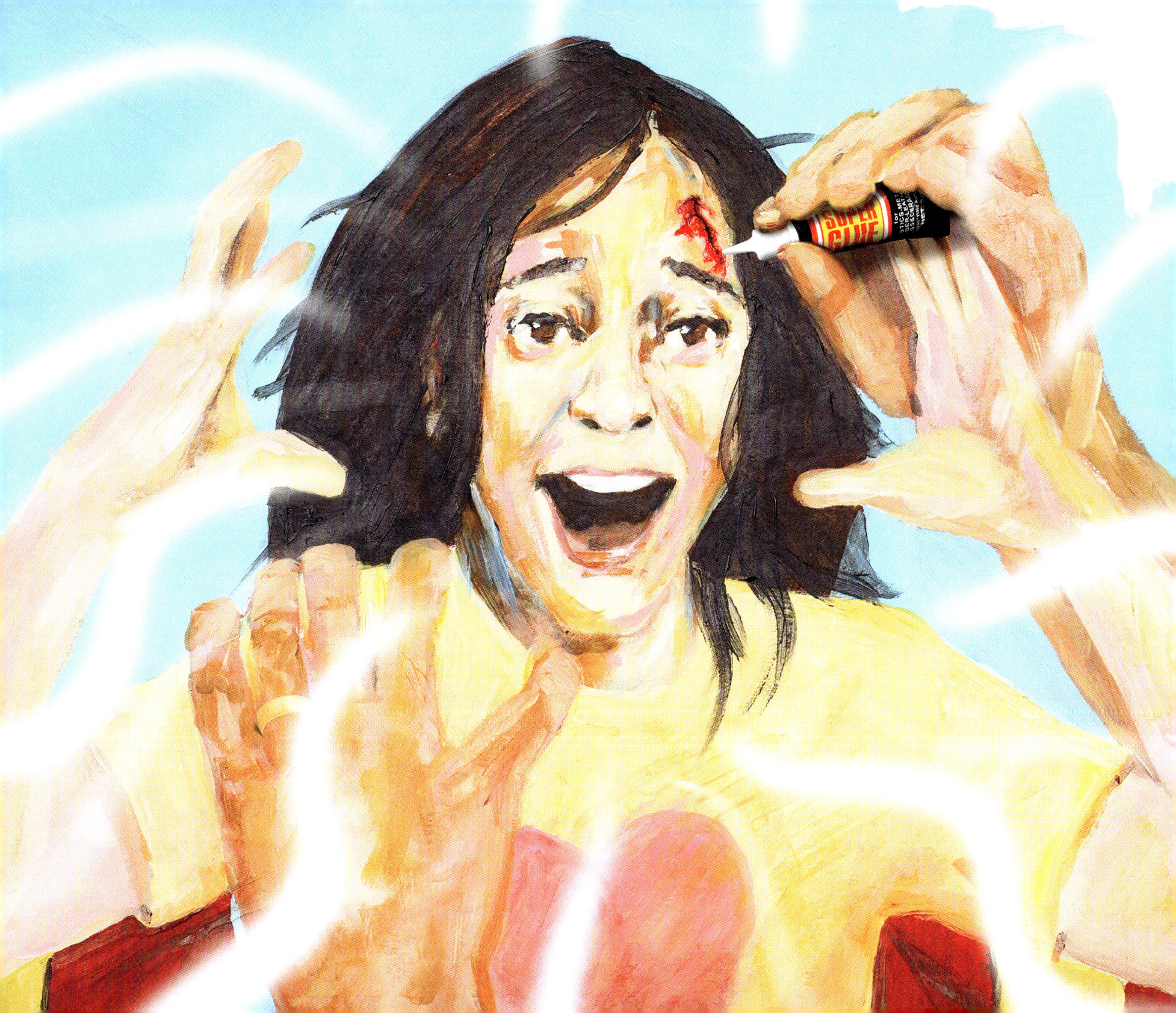
SUPER
GLUE

GOLD & SILVER
RA de
ONEDAS
AMANTE
RELO
Colón
CASA ASIA
COMPRAMOS ORO Y PLATA
EL BARATERO
CASA ASIA 505
507
gene
perfu

Before I knew it, we were in **Abuela's** station wagon. I leaned my head and freshly glued wound next to the window as the changing places dashed by like a movie in the distance.

Our small border town of La Union was nestled between three states and two countries.

And because of this, it was not long before the wagon made its way to El Paso, where **Abuelo** grew up.

I tried to imagine what he was like as a little boy. Born in the middle of the Great Depression, **Abuela** said that **Abuelo** had to start working when he was just a few years older than me.

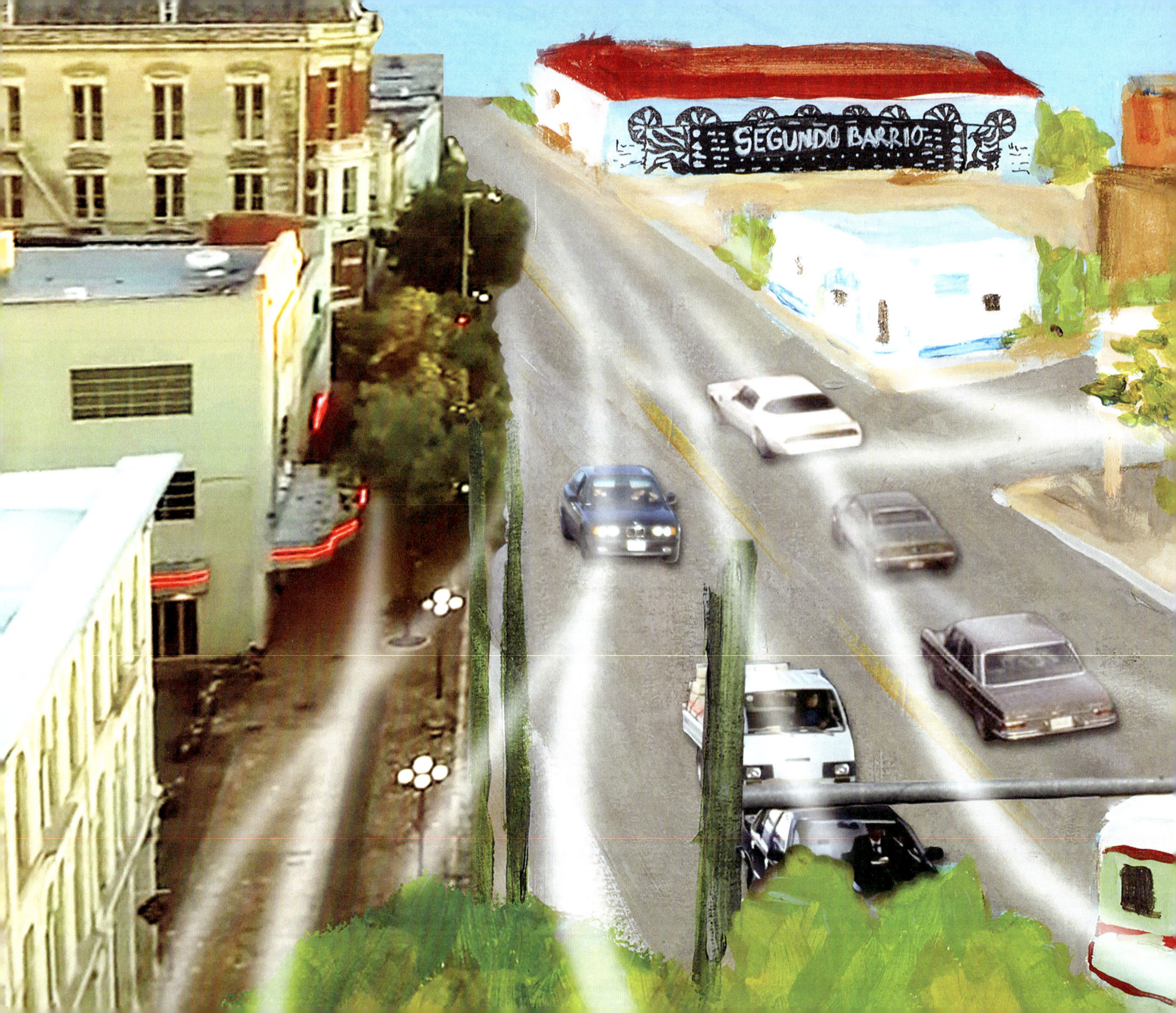
SEGUNDO BARRIO

He grew up in Segundo Barrio, in the city center where little boys like him had to work.

Back then, there were no walls, and Border people crossed back and forth freely.

Some families were here when this land was Mexico. Some families were here even longer before. Many, many families were here before the Pilgrims landed at Plymouth Rock and even before Spain occupied this land. Like our family, some Border families were the Indigenous peoples who roamed the land. And like our family, many families never left the Border. The Border and its wall came to us.

To many, the Border people became known as Mexican Americans. Like **Abuelo**, many proudly served their family's new country.

"This land went through many changes, **Mija**," **Abuelo** said.

"**Mira, Mija, Abuela** used to work here when she was young," **Abuelo** said, pointing to an old building downtown as we drove by.

"¿Really, **Abuelo**?" I asked, imagining what Abuela was like when she was young.

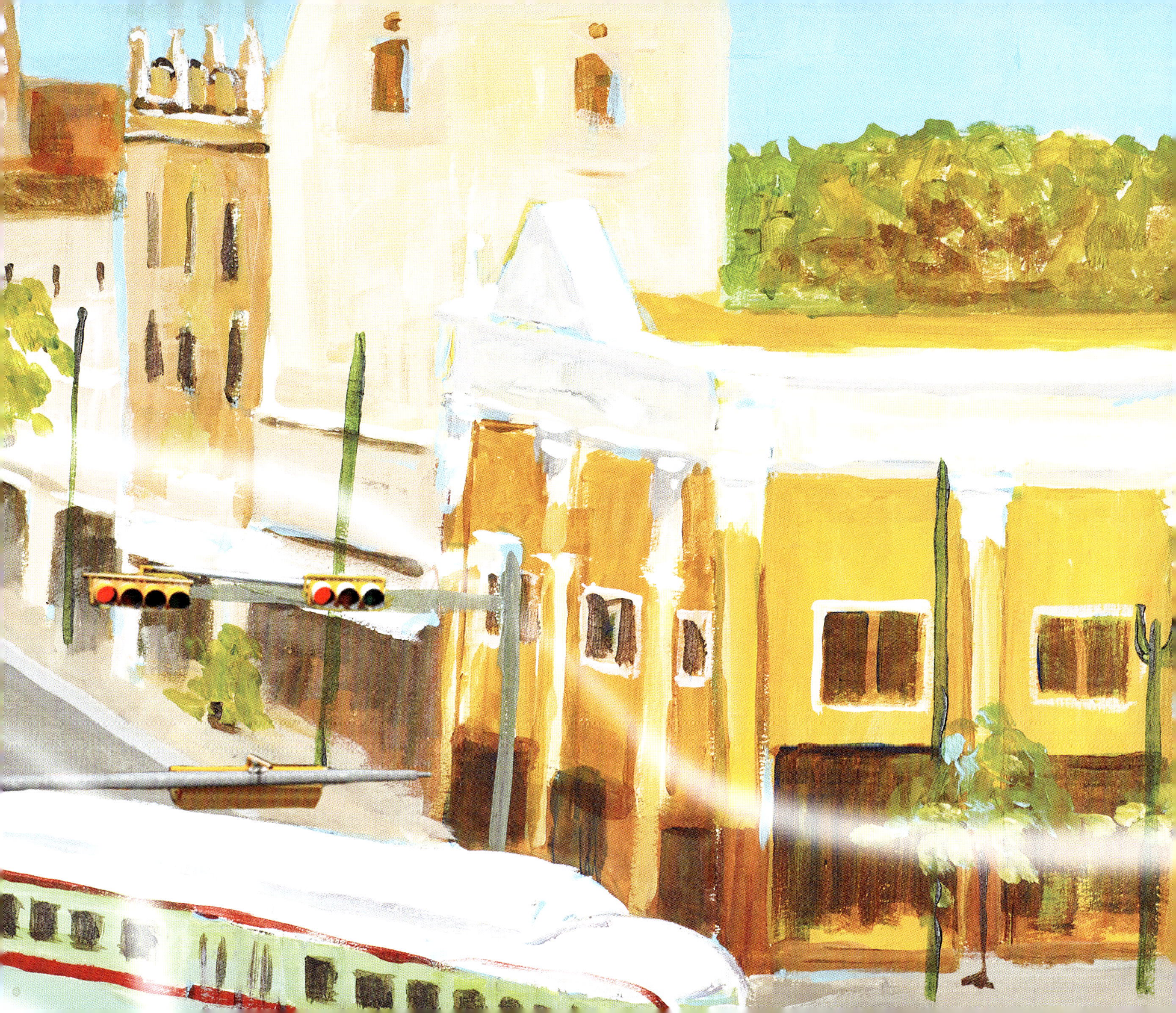

"Abuela was a good Catholic girl," Abuelo said.

Many people asked her to say prayers for their loved ones. Abuela would write their names on small slips of paper. Then, she lovingly tucked them in her Bible.

Abuela prayed for the sick, the wounded, the old, the needy, the poor, and the military.

At work, a young man gave her many names of soldiers from the Border to pray for.

Abuela was very serious about her prayers. She prayed to God that if her soldiers returned to the Border safely, she would make a pilgrimage to Mt. Cristo Rey each year.

Mike C. Pena
Rivera
Roberto Sierra
Ambrosio Guillen
dolfo P. Hernandez
Jesus Rodriguez
Eugene Arnold Obregon
Garcia
Joe R. Ba
Raul Alvarez d
Bald

Not far from where **Abuela** worked, **Abuelo** parked the station wagon, "This is El Segundo Barrio, **Mija**," he said.

I watched as **Abuelo** closed the door and made his way to my side of the wagon. Then, we walked small hand in big hand down Park Street until we reached El Bowie Bakery.

LA TIENDITA
IRMA
MILK
SODAS
BEER TO GO
thanks to all the talente
who collaborated on this
Susie Cortez
Simon Lopez (photog
Taylor Higginbotham (graphic a
Melissa Adams (digita
& Laura De la Torre (production a

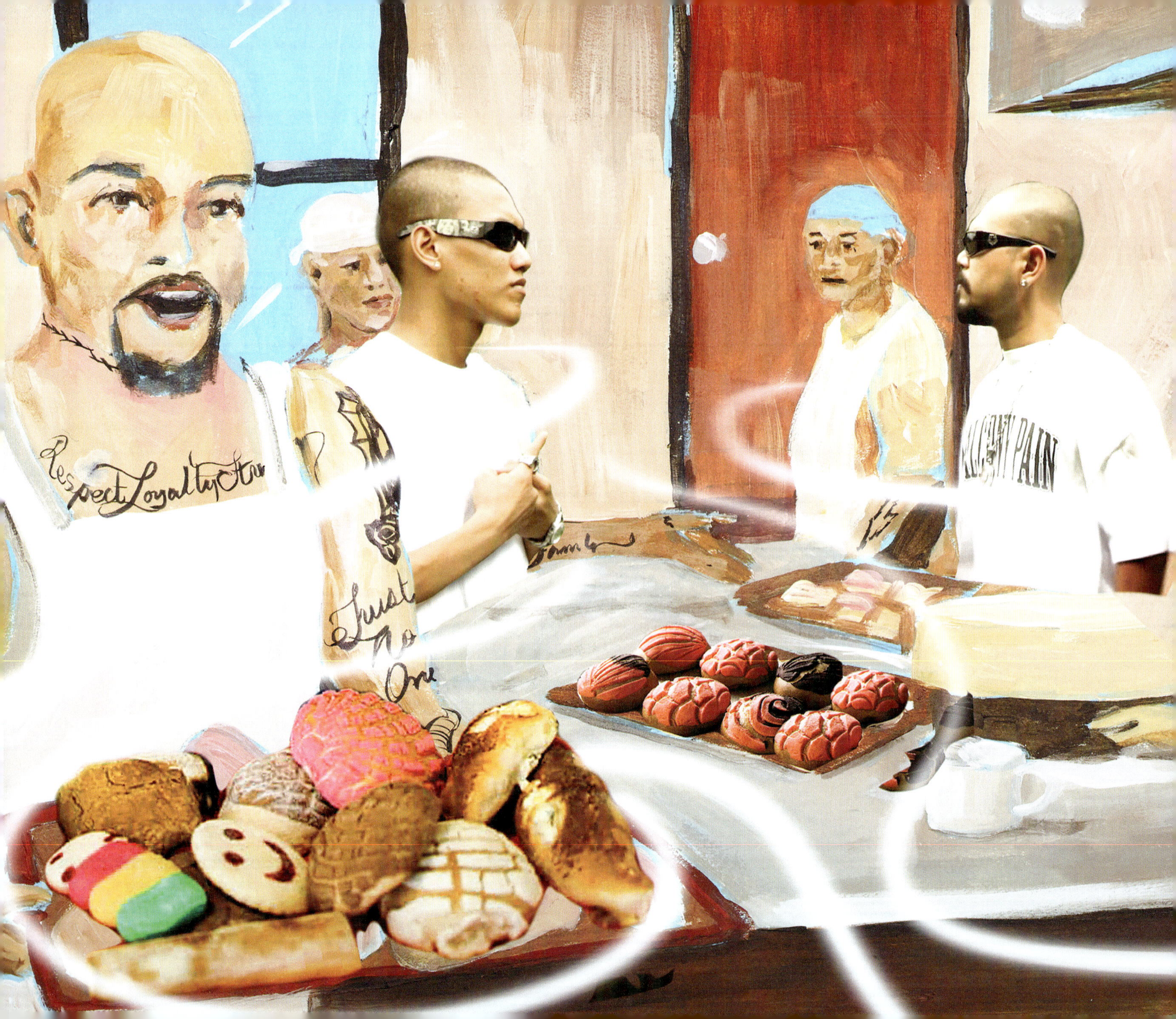
Respect Loyalty
PAIN

The bells rang as Abuelo opened the door to the bustling bakery, and the smell of pan dulce swirled through the air and made its way to my heart.

Local boys were cleaning tables, baking bread, and running the cash register.

"¡Don Poncho!" They shouted. I never heard Abuelo greeted with the ultimate title of respect. Abuelo casually responded with a big smile and lean, "Órale..."

"Mi nieta," Abuelo said, nudging me forward with pride. Then, each young man came over, one by one, to shake my hand.

"Andalé, Mija, go pick out your pan dulce. Get enough para todos para mañana," he instructed.

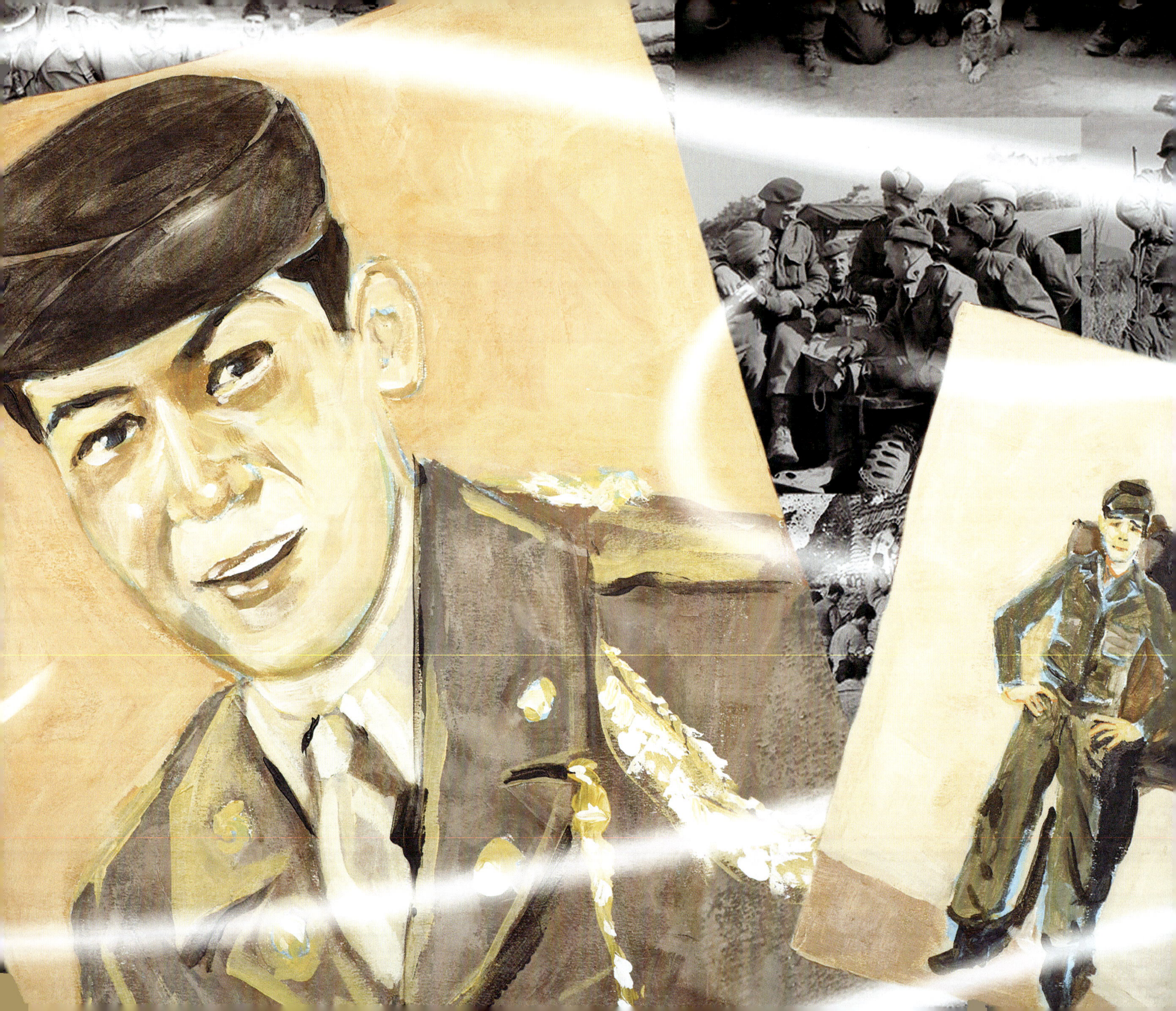

Shortly after **Abuelo** returned from the war, his friend got him a job at the same factory where **Abuela** worked.

It was love at first sight, and a year later, they got married.

One more year after that, **mi Papá**, **tu Abuelo** was born.

Miguel A. Vera
Mike C. Pena
Demensio Rivera
Joseph C. Rodriguez
Juan E. Negrón
Roberto Sierra
Victor H. Espinoza
Ambrosio Guillen
Rodolfo P. Hernandez
Bartolome Garcia
Jesus Rodriguez
Eduardo C. Gomez
Baldomero Lopez
Fernando Luis Garcia

Alfonso Castillo Muñoz

And that same year, while saying his prayers one night with **mi Abuela's** Bible, a small piece of paper fell out. **Mi Abuelo** knelt to pick it up. The paper read, "Alfonso Castillo Muñoz."

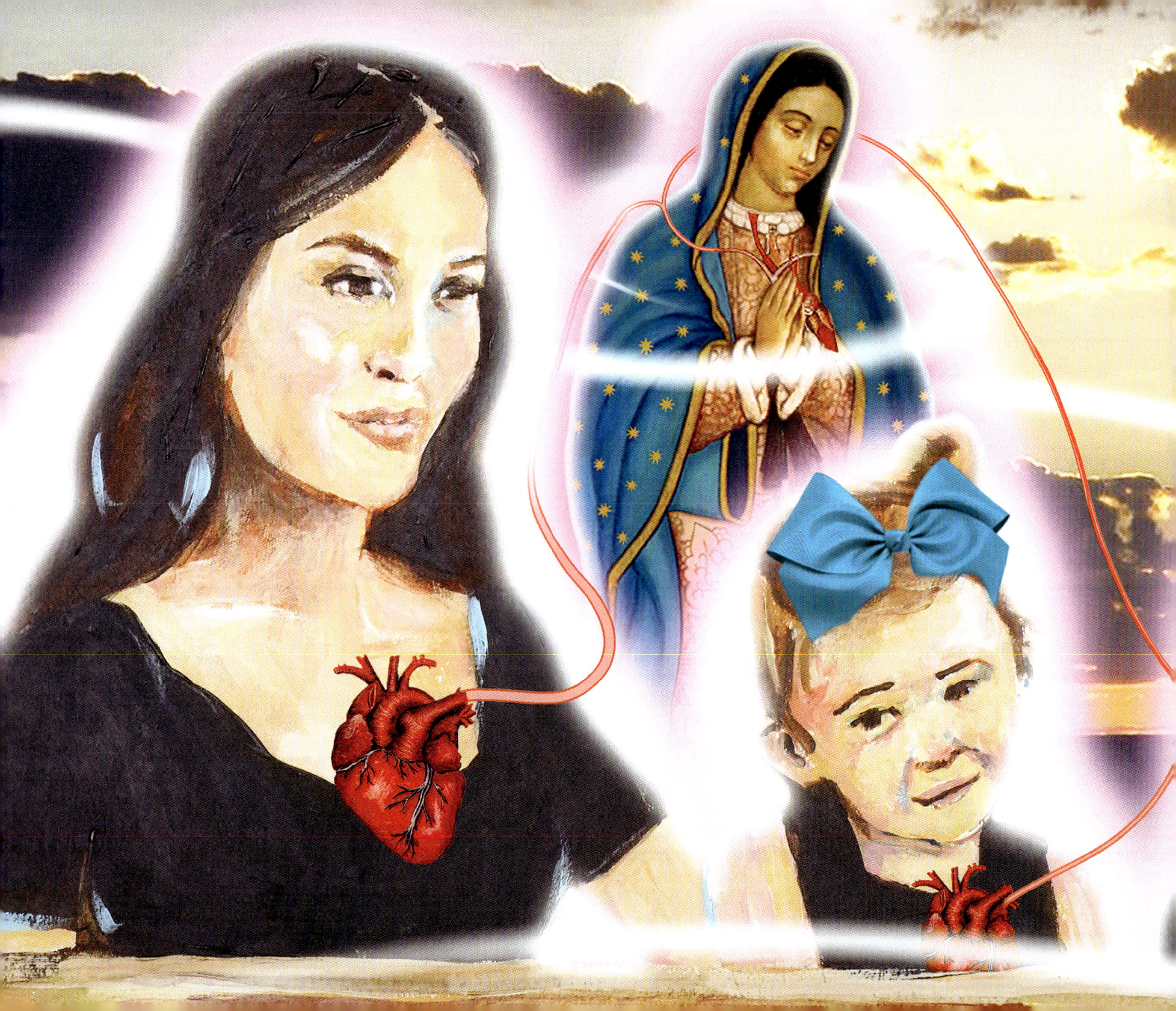

"Who is that, Mamá?"

"Well, that was **mi Abuelo's** real name, sweet girl. **Abuelo** never knew that **Abuela** had been praying for him."

The Alfonso she prayed for was the **Poncho Abuela** married.

"And when **Abuela** returned from her mission trip, the three of us made our annual pilgrimage to give thanks. We walked the winding road of Mt. Cristo Rey, sharing stories and eating **pan dulce** from El Bowie Bakery.

"This is the story of **mis Abuelos**, Girls.

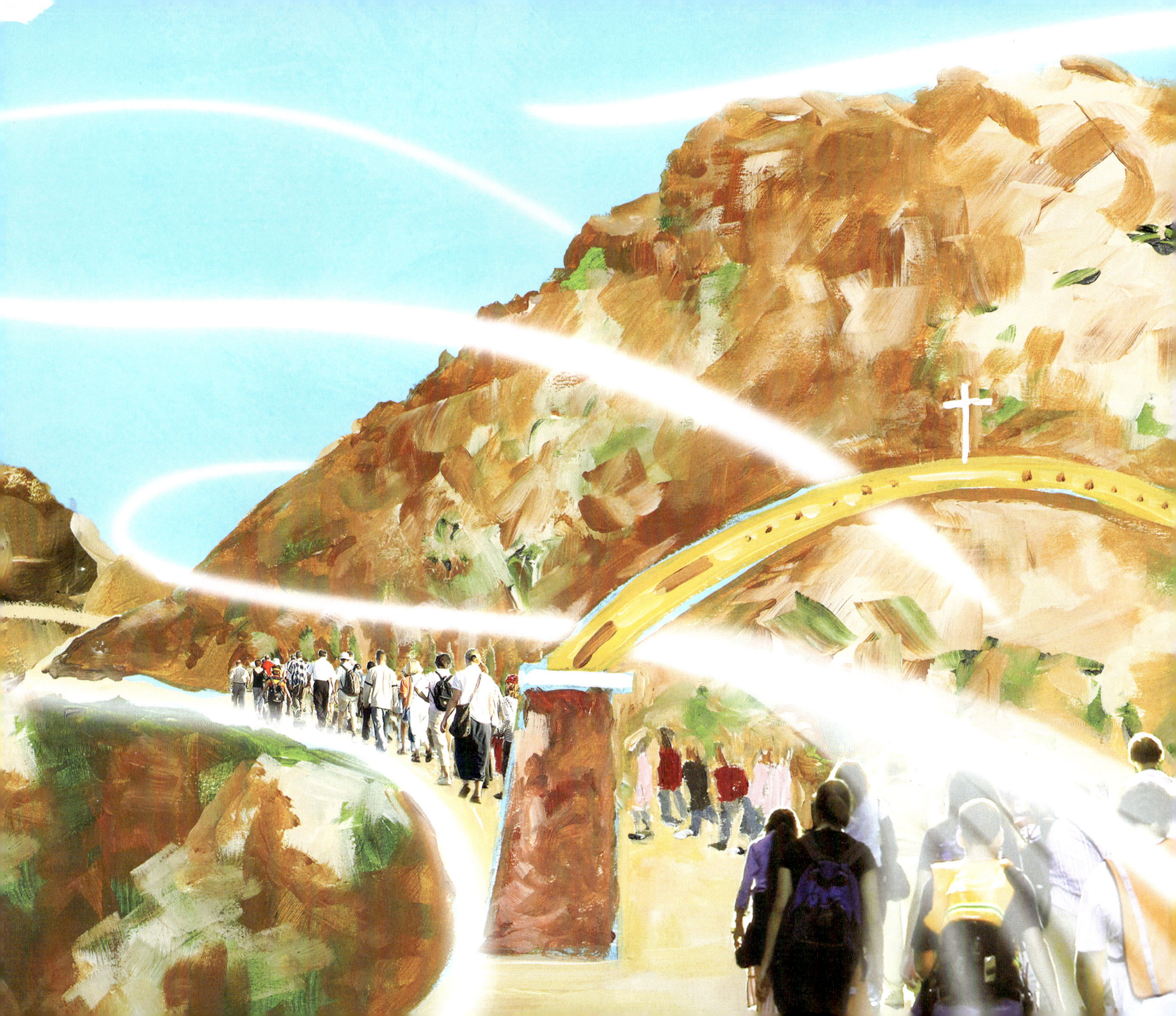

But now, this story belongs to the both of you. This is the story of **tus Bisabuelos**," I said touching the laps of my two little burritos.

"And today, Girls, we say goodbye to **Bisabuelo**. He may no longer be with us, but his stories and our memories will live on forever.

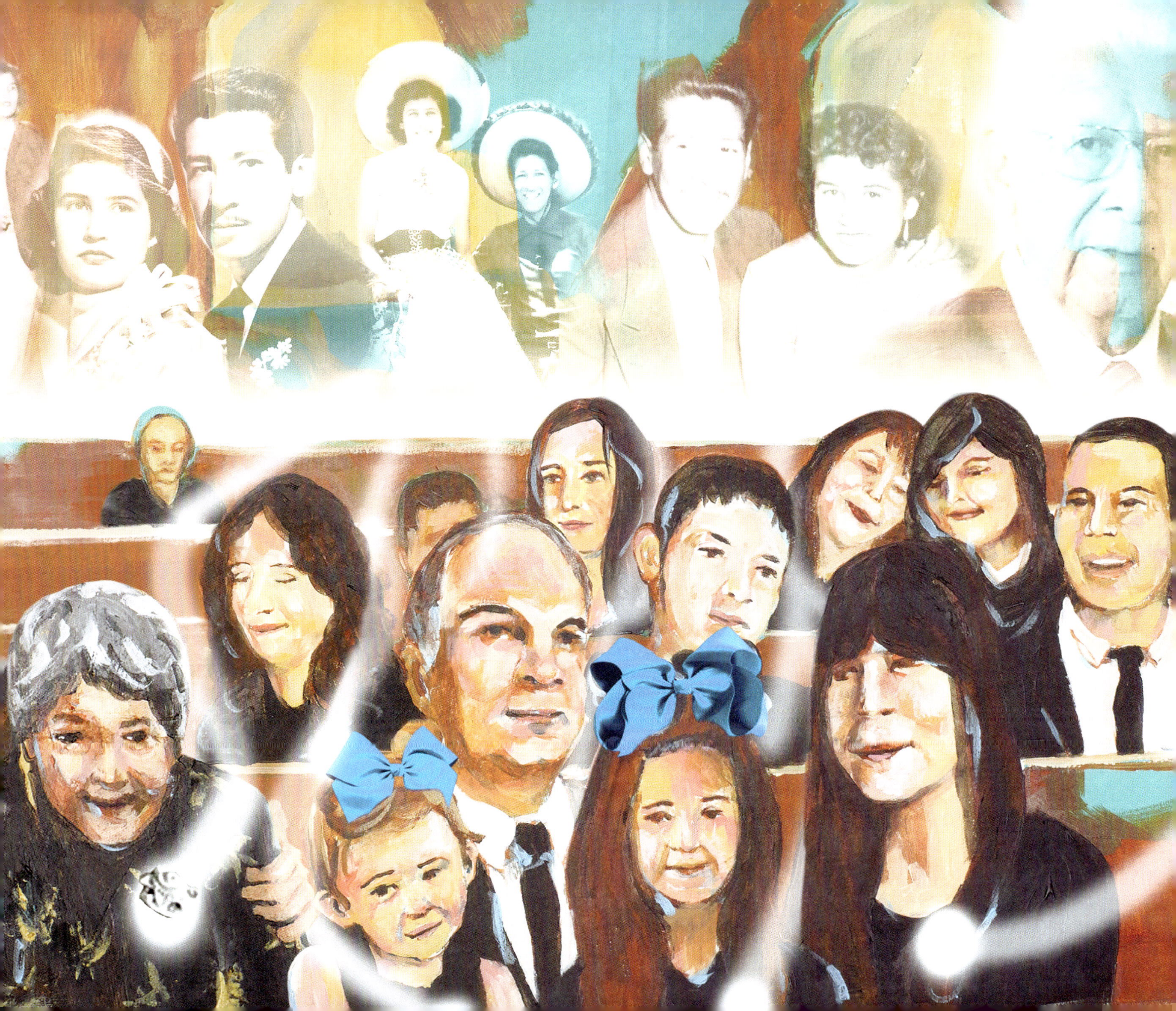

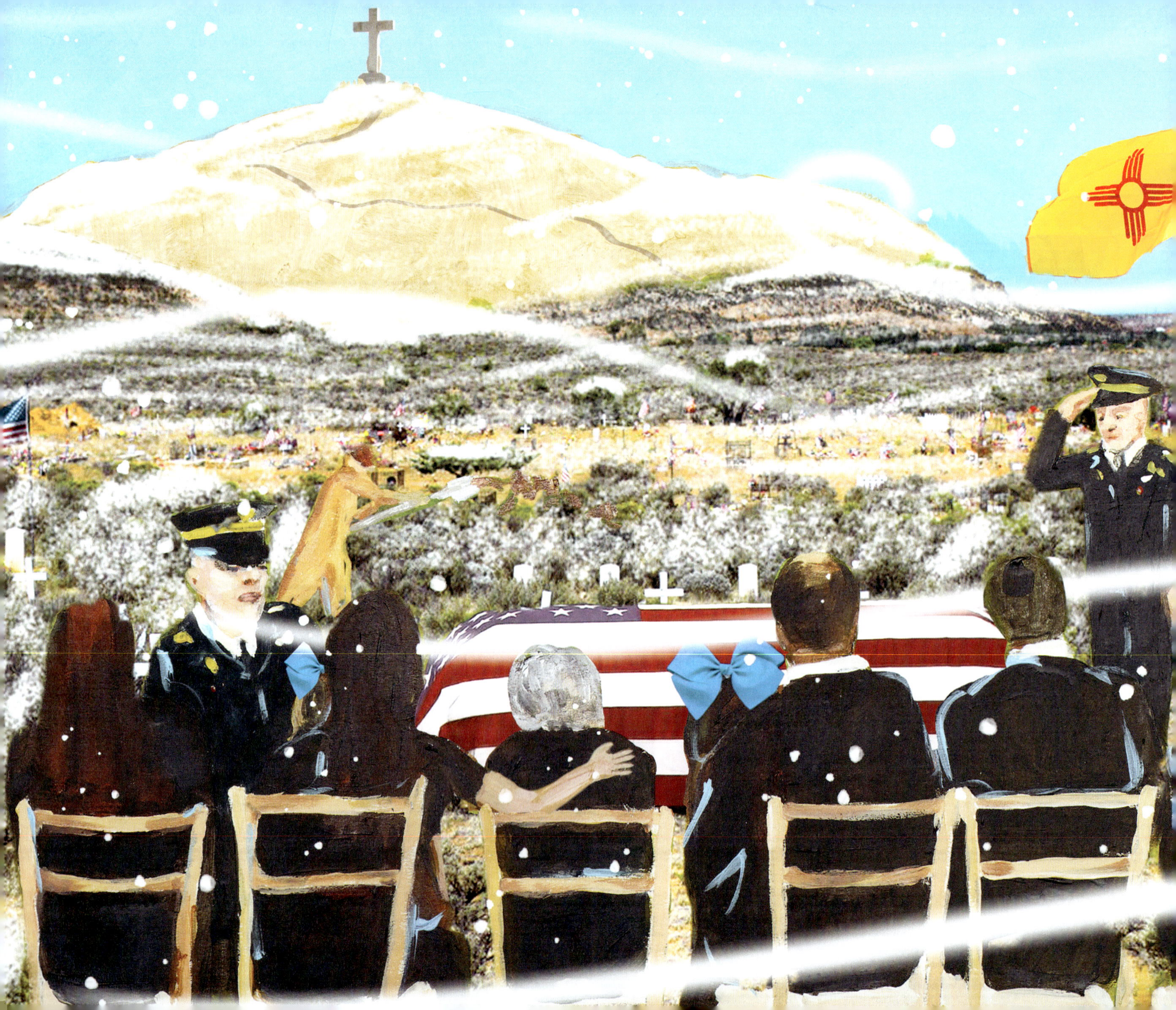

The sound of *la tierra* returned to the earth, gently covering a man who loved his family, his land, and his country. As one soldier played the trumpet softly in the background, another one folded the flag and presented it to *Abuela*.

I heard her whisper, "*¡Dios te bendiga!*" With my arms wrapped tightly around her, I clutched a small paper and my memories of *mi Abuelo*—Alfonso Castillo Muñoz.

El Fin

## About the Author

Visiting Assistant Professor, Director of CUSLAI (Center for U.S.-Latin America Initiatives), and Mellon Fellow at The University of Texas at Dallas, Muñoz's work focuses on a distinct population within the Latinx community. In 2020, she established the Community Digital Archive Project to reclaim the histories of that distinct community of multi-generational families and Indigenous peoples along the U.S.-Mexico Border. In her free time, you can catch Toni and her daughters, Darlington and Tennyson, embarking on RV road-tripping adventures.